In Love Again & Making It Work

SUCCESSFUL REMARRIAGE

Dick Dunn

DISCIPLESHIP RESOURCES

PO BOX 340003 • NASHVILLE, TN 37203-0003
www.discipleshipresources.org

ISBN 978-0-88177-534-1
Library of Congress Control Number 2008920848

Table of Contents

A Theology of Remarriage

emarriage is not exactly a new phenomenon. One hundred years ago stepfamilies were being created at about the same rate they are today, but for a different reason. In the past, remarriage usually followed the death of a mate, with many women dying during childbirth and men dying in work-related accidents and war. Today, the number of remarriages can largely be attributed to the high divorce rate.

Of course, many stepfamilies are still created due to the remarriage of someone who has been widowed. Working with single adults for many years, I am very aware of the large number of widowed singles of all ages in every community. Remarriage for the widowed, however, has never posed a theological problem for Christians. Remarriage has always been an acceptable option for the widowed. On the other hand, divorce and subsequent remarriage do pose serious problems for many Christians.

The difficulties Christians have with divorce and remarriage are due to the biblical teachings on these subjects. Jesus himself spoke very directly and pointedly about divorce. In The Sermon on the Mount, Jesus says, "But I say to you that anyone who divorces his wife, except on the ground of unchastity, causes her to commit adultery; and whoever marries a divorced woman commits adultery." (Matthew 5:32) Is it any wonder that many divorced Christians struggle with this issue concerning divorce and remarriage?

Having been divorced and remarried myself, I know the struggle divorced Christians go through as they read and hear the various passages of Scripture on these subjects. Not only do divorcing people experience the trauma of having their relational world torn apart, they also often feel a painful spiritual alienation from the church. Somehow, many kindly church persons, including some pastors, have a blind spot when it comes to divorce. How often I have heard the remark, "People get divorced too easily today." However, in all of my years of working with divorced people, I have yet to meet anyone who had an *easy* divorce. Divorce is painful for everyone involved, even the person who seeks the divorce.

I find it interesting that words of Jesus, which were obviously spoken out of his deep compassion for the plight of divorced women in his day, could in our day be turned around and used legalistically against both women and men. The social context of Jesus' teaching about divorce was a patriarchal system that allowed a man to divorce a woman, not in a court of law but simply in front of witnesses. It was his right simply for being a man. In the patriarchal world, women were possessions. Isn't it amazing that in many weddings we still go through the act of a father *giving* the bride to the husband?

There were two schools of thought on the subject of divorce at the time of Jesus. The school of Hillel said that it was a man's right to divorce his wife for anything that displeased him. The school of Shammai felt that this was too harsh, and limited a man's right to divorce only to situations in which the wife had been sexually unfaithful to the man.

The Gospel of Matthew tells a story of Pharisees trying to test Jesus by asking him, "Is it lawful for a man to divorce his wife for any cause?" Matthew 19:3. The same story when told in Mark leaves off the phrase *for any cause* and simply asks, "Is it lawful for a man to divorce his wife?" Mark 10:2. If one follows the story in Matthew, it would seem that Jesus makes a choice between the two schools of Hillel and Shammai by choosing that of Shammai and indicating that the only legitimate reason for a man to divorce his wife was adultery—her adultery not his. Mark, on the other hand, does not equivocate. According to the story in Mark, Jesus says that divorce is wrong—period.

Since according to the story, the Pharisees are testing Jesus, the test is obviously to get Jesus to choose sides and alienate one group against him. Therefore, I suspect that Mark has told the story more accurately. As he does in so many other situations, Jesus offers a third alternative—namely, that divorce is wrong no matter the cause.

There is no getting around the truth that God hates divorce (see Malachi 2:16). For that matter, almost all divorced people also hate divorce. It was not what they intended or expected when they married. Some people seem to think that in our day and time people get married with the idea that if it doesn't work out, they will simply get divorced. However, I have yet to meet a couple that married with such a thought.

What we often fail to understand is that God not only hates divorce, **God also hates a marriage that is not fulfilling its purpose.** Marriage is meant to help husband, wife, and all children become all that God intended for them to be. Divorce needs to be compared with a bad marriage, not a good one. Neither divorce nor a bad marriage is the will of God.

God only desires good marriages. Often, marriages that are not functioning well can be repaired. When that is possible, certainly it should be done. When it is not possible, however, divorce can be like surgery. It will leave scars on everyone involved, but it can allow for people to put their lives back together and be redeemed. We must also remember that it takes two people working together to make a good marriage. It really only takes one person to make a divorce. If one person decides to stop trying, the marriage cannot succeed to fulfill God's will.

In the patriarchal world of Jesus' day, the plight of a divorced woman was very bad. Following being divorced, if a woman was fortunate, she might be able to go back to her parents, if they were still alive and in a position to take her back, or she might be able to marry again. If she was less fortunate, there were not very many alternatives to becoming a prostitute. I have often wondered if Jesus' compassion for the prostitutes was simply because he saw the plight of divorced women.

I doubt that God approves of divorce any more today than in the days of Jesus. That is not God's intention for marriage. However, the social context has changed a little. It is not surprising that the divorce rate started climbing at the point in time when a woman could survive economically apart from the support of a man. While parity has certainly not been achieved, survival has.

Divorce and remarriage may not be what God intended. However, they are not unforgivable sins. God does not cast off those who have failed at marriage and then seek to try again. I can personally attest that my faith has grown significantly since my divorce in 1977 and my remarriage in 1982. I have seen similar growth among hundreds of others. God is constantly seeking to redeem his children.

We have a long way to go in our world in order to fulfill God's plan for marriage. Helping people make successful marriages must be our goal. Subsequent marriages can succeed with a little help.

Introduction

$\mathscr{F}$or a subsequent marriage to have a good chance for success, certain things need to happen prior to the marriage. Hoping for a successful marriage without these is like trying to bake a cake with only part of the ingredients. You are certain to end up with something, but it is not likely to resemble what you intended or hoped for.

When asked about what chance people had for successful subsequent marriages, I once heard someone remark, "With or without help?" To her, it made all the difference whether or not a couple was going to try it on their own, or admit from the start that subsequent marriages are difficult and need all the help they can get. I certainly agree that stepfamily couples need help.

Living in a subsequent marriage myself, I am constantly aware of just how different this marriage is from my first one. In many ways, it is so much better—more than I ever could have imagined. After all, I am older and better able to appreciate the things we do together and what we offer one another. I am even able to enjoy my wife as an individual so totally different from myself and not be threatened by those differences. In this marriage, I am relaxed, confident, hopeful, and extremely happy—even though there are times when I am none of these.

It has taken us several years to reach this place. The first two or three years were frequently tumultuous. There were periods during those early years when I was sure that I would soon be numbered among those who had failed at marriage more than once, which probably would have happened if we had not received help.

The truth is that **most subsequent marriages fail.** The obstacles involved are massive. Without experience to draw upon, most of us get in over our heads without any understanding of what to do or how to do it. I thank God that Betty and I had someone to talk with during those times. The question, "With or without help?" makes a lot of sense to me.

At first, we had an individual counselor. Later, we developed a support group for people in subsequent marriages and discovered that our story was not unique. In fact, most people in such marriages share our story. Those early years can be and usually are difficult, but they are not impossible. With even a little help, most of the obstacles quickly become stepping stones upon which to build a wonderful future.

Therefore, today when I talk with couples seeking to enter subsequent marriages, I ask for two things at the very beginning:

First—I ask for a commitment to **not even consider divorce during the first three years of the marriage.** I have found that if a couple will stick it out for at least three years, the issues they struggled with up till then will usually be resolved, the stepfamily relationships will have improved considerably, and their marriage will have a good chance of becoming the exciting relationship they anticipated at the beginning.

Second—I ask them to **agree to seek counseling whenever the other person thinks they need it.** Seldom do both feel the need at the same time.

Subsequent marriages can be wonderful. This will not just happen, however. It will take much work. It will take much prayer. It will take much patience. And, it will take all the love and understanding anyone can give. Actually, that is what makes it wonderful. As couples work together to make their marriage succeed, each person comes to a greater appreciation for the person they married. Truths about marriage never known before are discovered, and the marriage grows accordingly.

Questions

1. Do each of you hereby commit that you will not even consider divorce in the first three years of your marriage?

2. Will you agree to seek counseling together at any time in the marriage your partner feels you need it? You will be asked to reconfirm this decision in Section Four, Chapter Four where the idea is explored more fully.

Section One

Being Ready

CHAPTER ONE

When Infatuation Passes

*M*arriage relationships in our culture all begin with a time of *falling in love*. During this time of infatuation the other person is not really perceived as a different person apart from oneself but as a mere extension of one's own being. It is a time full of illusions and fantasies, having little to do with reality. Dating couples actually contribute to the fantasy by not being totally honest with each other but by being what each believes the other desires. Marrying during the infatuation period of a relationship means marrying not an individual but a fantasy that will ultimately disappear.

Take for example Ira and Cynthia. Ira loved basketball and it was quite natural when he met Cynthia to invite her to a basketball game. Although she really hated basketball, Cynthia liked Ira and accepted his invitation. They had a good time that night and Cynthia found that she enjoyed the game more than she expected, probably because she was with Ira. A few days later, Cynthia invited Ira to join her at a horse show. While Ira decided to join her, he had always found horse shows to be very boring—a rodeo would have been fine, but a horse show— well, since it was Cynthia he would try it. Interestingly enough, he had fun.

Both Ira and Cynthia had no idea that the other did not share their particular interest, and it was only much later that either felt comfortable enough to say so. Is it any wonder that dating people get confused?

Studies have shown that in many ways the experience of *falling in love* is a return to infancy, at least in feeling. At birth, a baby is unable to distinguish that mother and father are not simply extensions of itself. Just as an infant learns to control its fingers, it also learns how to get these bigger extensions of its being (the parents) to do things like pick it up, feed it, and change its diapers by crying, cooing, or smiling. As adults, we realize that infants believing they can control others this way is simply an illusion. It usually takes an infant about a year or two to begin to understand that parents and others are separate beings. Then the baby begins to devise other ways to get mother or father to do what it wants. That is why we call this time *the terrible twos.*

As adults, it is obvious that an infant is a totally helpless creature. However, without experience yet to understand this truth, the child sees this time as one of great power. In most situations, all it has to do is cry or make some other noises and its wishes are quickly fulfilled. How much more powerful can one get?

When we fall in love, many of these ancient feelings return. We think, "Here is someone who really understands and accepts me just as I am. He or she likes the same things I do. We think alike! Frequently, we respond to one another before the desire is expressed. We are on the same wavelength. There is nothing we cannot do together. No obstacle is too big, no problem is too difficult!"

Do you see how similar this sort of thinking is to that of a newly born infant? I have had couples come to see me about getting married, and as we talked, all I could see were the tremendous struggles that lay ahead for them. Sometimes, there were several children from their previous marriages. Sometimes, there were severe economic problems. Sometimes, there were in-law situations or problems with former spouses that would make even the greatest optimist cringe. Yet, these people were *in love,* and to them, all of these situations seemed like only minor irritations that could be easily overcome.

The period of infatuation is like that. It is a time filled with illusion. But just as the illusion of an infant thinking it was all-powerful and that mother and father were simply extensions of itself was false, the illusions of infatuation are equally false. **Eventually, all illusions**

give way to reality. It is far better that this happens before people marry rather than after.

People in love view the future from a state of consciousness altered by the intoxicating affects of romance. Eventually, it becomes clear that the beloved is not a carbon copy of oneself in the form of the opposite sex. He or she does not think the same thoughts. They do not even like all of the same things. Their sexual desires are not always in sync. Being separate individuals, they have as many differences as they have similarities.

Infatuation will pass, and only as it does can partners learn the other dimensions of love. As long as they are madly (an appropriate word) *in love* they have not begun to understand and appreciate the other person as she or he actually is.

Questions

1. Describe what falling in love with your partner was like. In what ways has that changed? In what ways is the feeling still the same?

2. In what ways is your partner similar to you? In what ways is your partner very different from you?

3. How do you handle times when you disagree with your partner? How does he or she react to disagreements? How are differences resolved?

CHAPTER TWO

Mourning Past Relationships

*A*ll subsequent marriages are born out of grief. Either a previous mate has died or there has been a divorce, which means the previous marriage has died. Both situations need to be mourned. A subsequent marriage is like a phoenix rising out of the ashes of a past marriage.

This does not mean that someone should just sit around waiting for this grief period to end. Nothing could be further from the truth. The time of grief is a good period in which to develop close friendships with people of both sexes, especially with other single people. However, the grief period is a time for **friendship**, not **romance**. Friendships will teach far more about what someone desires in relationships. After a good network of single friends has been established, both the divorced and widowed will be much more relaxed and content, as well as far better prepared to make a wise choice in a marriage partner.

Both Robert and Becky felt miserable after each became suddenly single, Robert being widowed and Becky being divorced. They met one day at the supermarket. Chatting about which cut of meat was best, Robert invited Becky to dinner. They hit it off immediately, and each felt the other was an answer to their prayers. The pain and loneliness had lessened, and for the first time since Robert's wife had died and Becky's husband had left, both felt that perhaps life could still have meaning.

The problem with becoming romantically involved at such a time is that the biggest thing about the couple right then is what is missing. Robert missed his wife more than anything. Without her, he felt like he had nothing to live for. When Becky's husband left, this once self-assured woman shriveled and doubted that she could do anything worthwhile. Both were very lonely. Much of what pulled them together was the emptiness they both felt.

However, emptiness passes. Unless a relationship is built upon positives rather than negatives, their togetherness will have little to sustain it after the mourning period has ended. That is not to say that people ever *get over* the death of a mate or that anyone ever *gets over* a divorce. These events remain for a lifetime. People do move through the period of intense grief though, and this needs to occur **prior** to a subsequent marriage, not after.

In the case of Becky and Robert, they fortunately put off marriage and decided that if they still felt love for each other after a year, they would talk about marriage then. As both began to heal from their losses, however, their feelings changed, and they stopped seeing one another.

Questions

1. How long have you been widowed or divorced? If you have been neither divorced nor widowed, are you presently recovering from any other grief experiences?

2. Where in the grief process would you place both yourself and your partner?

3. Describe what the grief experience has been like for you. What was the worst part of it? What are some things that helped?

4. What was the kindest thing anyone did for you during your grief?

CHAPTER THREE

Forgiveness

*I*t is almost impossible to experience either the death of a mate or a divorce and not struggle with both anger and guilt. Both of these emotions are very useful if handled correctly, but both guilt and anger can become very destructive if not used well.

Imagine what it would be like to live without emotions. You could neither be happy nor sad, angry nor glad, and neither peaceful nor worried. You would experience life but not feel it. What a horrible existence! God gave us all of our emotions for a purpose, including those emotions with which we are often uncomfortable. Anger and guilt are two of these uncomfortable emotions.

Anger is a gift from God. Anger comes when we have been hurt, and it gives us the energy and power to take action to protect ourselves. When we get angry, even our body chemistry changes with an infusion of adrenaline. Sometimes people have the mistaken notion that they should never get angry. However, anger is one of God's blessings—not a curse. Anger only becomes a problem when it gets out of control.

Rachel became very angry when her husband left her for another woman. She wanted to hurt him as much as he had caused her pain. At the same time, she felt internal conflict because she had been taught that she was supposed to "turn the other cheek."

Of course, Jesus never meant for his followers to allow themselves to be abused. Jesus himself stood up to his detractors on numerous occasions. However, what Jesus was instructing his followers to do was not use their anger to seek to destroy and pay back someone who had hurt them.

Rachel's anger was indeed a blessing. It allowed her to take action so as not to continue being hurt. It would have been wrong, however, to try to pay her husband back. She needed to use her anger to supply the energy to move on with her life.

Guilt is another emotion with which the suddenly single often wrestle. Whether a person is widowed or divorced, feeling guilty is a common emotion. Some guilt comes because we have done wrong, but we also often feel guilt falsely. The person who says, "Surely there must have been something I could have done to prevent this," is probably feeling false guilt.

Guilt frequently causes people to do things they would not ordinarily do—things they know they should not do but feel compelled to do. Guilt can interfere with any subsequent relationship and should not be a part of a subsequent marriage. Former spouses will cause plenty of headaches in subsequent marriages, even very stable ones. If one of the partners is filled with guilt over something unresolved in the previous marriage, that guilt can create great strain in a new one.

Non-custodial parents often feel guilty over their inability to adequately parent their children who reside primarily with the former spouse. Frequently, they compensate for their lack of time by buying the children many things or by taking them to exciting places. This is not good parenting and will only create problems. Some non-custodial parents become so frustrated with not being able to parent like they desire that they pull back from their children, seeing them less and less. While such behavior might be understandable, children really do need both parents deeply involved in their lives as much as possible. Neither guilt nor frustration makes for good parenting. Both need to be resolved rather than brought into a new family.

Both anger and guilt can be resolved by forgiveness. When we forgive someone who has wronged us, it frees us from the pain and permits us to move on. When we refuse to forgive, it holds the pain within and gives the person who wronged us continuing power over us. **Forgiveness is always more for our own good than for the other person.**

Guilt is also resolved by forgiveness—the forgiveness of ourselves. Sometimes forgiving ourselves is more difficult than forgiving others. Nevertheless, we need and deserve forgiveness as much as anyone else. One aspect of our humanity is that we will mess up. None of us is perfect. Even if we try our best (and none of us does that all the time), we will fail often. Rather than feeling guilty, we need to acknowledge our failures, determine to do better, and then move on by forgiving ourselves for our mistakes.

Questions

1. How frequently do you communicate with the person to whom you were previously married? What do you talk about? What is the usual result?

2. How do you *feel* when you talk with him or her? After you finish the conversation, how do you *feel?* What do you usually do?

3. Are you aware of any feelings of guilt concerning this person? Over what do you feel guilty?

4. Does this person use your guilt to get what she or he wants from you? If so, how?

CHAPTER FOUR

Internet Dating

*M*any couples preparing for marriage today have met over the internet. The internet provides a convenient way to meet people and "chat" about almost anything and everything. Even shy people can comfortably communicate with others from the security of their own homes. Internet dating is simply a lot easier than trying to meet someone in public.

The major problem with internet dating, of course, is that none of us are quite the same in person as we are *online*. In the privacy of our homes, we do not need to dress up, look good, or even smell good. We can pretend to be anything we want. Until, that is, that we actually meet.

It is impossible not to project an image of the person we are dating on the internet into our minds. In the hours we spend writing back and forth, our minds create a mental picture of this person. Even though we may have sent pictures to each other over the internet, our minds create a much more detailed picture. Since we obviously desire companionship and want this person to be ideal for us, in part, we create what we desire.

The problem with internet dating is that without the person actually present, our minds do not have a filter of the little things we intuitively pick up in person. There is no body language on a computer monitor. There is no inflection in a person's voice. There is no interaction with other people. How that person will be with children is impossible to detect. Even if we have been talking on the phone, it can never be the same as actually being with that person.

Therefore, people who meet on the internet must take their time. **Internet dating is no substitute for person-to-person dating.** Although it may be a way to begin, only spending an adequate amount of time with this person and his or her family will allow reality to overshadow the mental picture created on line. Remember, marriage must be lived out in person, not on a computer screen.

How much time is adequate to really know another person? It depends a great deal upon the circumstances. Long-distance romances are extremely difficult. Eventually, one person is going to have to move. It is wiser to move prior to getting engaged and taking the time necessary to find out if this is something both really want than to marry and be disappointed later. Divorce is always painful.

When there are children, the children will need a considerable amount of time to even begin to be comfortable with a new person living with them, especially another parent figure. Keep in mind that the children have not been writing back and forth, nor have they been talking for hours on the phone. (Be sure to read Section Three relating to children and remarriage.)

Internet dating is here to stay. It may even become more popular as computers and cell phones become more technologically advanced. As long as people use reason and patience, internet dating can be a tool that brings couples together. However, the difficult task of moving past infatuation to a lasting relationship will still be up to the people involved.

Questions

1. Describe how you met. What were you feeling when you first "chatted?"

2. How long have you actually dated in person, face to face? How has that been different from dating *online*?

3. What was it like to meet for the first time? What were your fears? What were your hopes?

4. How has your mental picture of this person

changed from what you imagined she or he would be like?

5. How much time have you managed to spend with the children from your previous marriages? What has their reaction been?

CHAPTER FIVE

Adequate Pre-Marital Counseling

J believe that no one should marry without pre-marital counseling. Marriage is just too important a relationship to be entered into without fully considering the covenant being made. A marriage involving someone that has been married before and has children from the previous marriage makes pre-marital counseling all the more imperative. While how much pre-marital counseling is adequate may be open to debate, a minimum should include: 1) taking a pre-marital inventory such as *Prepare MC[1]* and talking with a counselor about the results, 2) reading at least one book about step-families, 3) talking with a couple in a stepfamily who has been married at least five years, and if possible, 4) attending a support group for couples in blending families. Let's look at each of these suggestions.

1. Life Innovations, Inc.; P.O. Box 190; Minneapolis, MN 55440; 800-331-1661.

Using a Pre-Marital Inventory

The *Prepare* inventory is certainly not the only such devise used by counselors to assist them in helping couples assess their relationship. It is simply the one with which I am best acquainted. *Prepare*, *Prepare MC* (married with children), and *Enrich* (for couples already married) are sets of 165 statements related to various aspects of the relationship. Separately, each of the partners indicates whether they "Strongly agree," "Agree," are "Undecided," "Disagree," or "Strongly disagree" with each of those statements. After filling in the inventory, these sheets are sent away to be scored. Two weeks later the counselor receives the results compiled in a way that he or she can then talk with the couple about the strengths and growth areas of the relationship.

Most couples are a little nervous about taking the premarital inventory. Many ask when they return, "Did we pass?" However, there is no pass or fail to it, and I have never had a couple that was not very happy that we used this instrument to help them create a vital marriage. I know from a counselor's point of view that I could never have obtained all the information provided on my own.

Books About Stepfamilies

Read at least one more book (besides this book) about stepfamilies. More and more is being written about the subject of blending families. Your local bookstore and library will have several. I will recommend to you one of my own, *Willing to Try Again: Steps Toward Blending a Family*[2]. Reading about the sort of issues you are likely to encounter will not prevent them from happening, but it will keep you from being blindsided when they hit. I know of several couples that have read a least half a dozen books about stepfamilies, and they really appreciate the help.

I would also suggest that you underline or highlight as you read in order that you can talk about the various issues with each other. Discussing these matters together will help you strengthen your couple relationship.

Talk With Successful Couples

Talk with a stepfamily couple who has been married at least five years. A couple who has "been there" will be able to help you understand what lies ahead. Their circumstance may not be exactly like yours but there are enough similarities in blending families that you will benefit from their experience. Plan to talk with them before the wedding and ask if you can talk with them at least a couple more times during your first year of marriage. They will help you see that what you are experiencing is very normal.

---

2. Dick Dunn, *Willing to Try Again: Steps Toward Blending a Family* (Judson Press, Valley Forge, PA, 1993).

Support Groups

Attend a stepfamily support group in your area. Depending on where you live, this may or may not be possible. I encourage every couple I marry where at least one of them has children from a previous marriage to attend our Stepfamily Support Group prior to getting married. Most of them do, and those who attend say they really benefit from the experience. Just hearing other couples talk about what blending a family is like will keep you from being surprised. To find a group in your area, check first with your own church. If they do not have a program, call several of the other churches in your community.

Your marriage is much more important than your wedding. Your wedding will take only a short amount of time. Hopefully, your marriage will last a lifetime. Preparation for your marriage should be more important than preparation for your wedding.

Questions

1. Who will do your pre-marital counseling? What pre-marital inventory does he or she use?

2. What book about stepfamilies do you plan to read?

3. What stepfamily couple do you plan to talk to about stepfamilies?

4. What stepfamily support groups exist in you area? When do you plan to attend?

Section Two

Practical Considerations

CHAPTER ONE

Where to Live

*A*part from convenience, many couples pay little attention as to where they will be living. In subsequent marriages, both partners often have homes, and the simplest thing is for one person to move in with the other, usually based upon whichever home is largest or more strategically located to where the couple works or the children go to school.

That is exactly what Joan and Harry did. After his divorce, Harry lived in an apartment that served his purposes fine. His two children, both boys, had a room that they shared when they came to see him. The rest of the time, Harry had the place to himself.

When he married Joan, Harry simply moved in with her. Joan had a home where she lived with her three children, two girls and a boy. Each of them had their own room, and Joan and Harry fixed up a space in a spare room off the family room where Harry's sons could sleep when they came. It certainly seemed like this was the perfect solution as to where they would live.

The only problem was that Harry (and his sons) always thought of it as Joan's house. Even after they had placed Harry's name on the deed along with Joan's, it still seemed like her place because she had lived there with her daughters before Harry moved in. Joan's children always had the sense that Harry and his sons had moved into *their* space. After three years, Harry and Joan decided to buy a new house where they could all begin fresh.

Unless one person's moving in with the other is the only practical solution (and sometimes it is), couples will be well advised to look for a place where neither lived before. There are two basic reasons for this:

First: If it is a home where one of you once lived with a former spouse (deceased or divorced), it will be filled with memories, both good and bad. While the person owning the home may have adjusted to these memories, it is frequently difficult for the new mate to live with such thoughts on a daily basis without feeling some jealousy and pain. If there are children involved, they will be accustomed to furniture and pictures having their proper place in the house, and the children are likely to resent any changes the new spouse may propose.

Second: When one person moves into another's home (even a home not previously shared with a former mate), there is a sense of ownership involved. The person who lived there before will have a difficult time not thinking of it as *my house*, while the person moving in will tend to think of the house as *yours*. These feelings may pass in time, but usually it takes many years for this to happen.

If at all possible, therefore, it is helpful to move into a house that is new to the couple and to any children involved. That way, it is your home together from the beginning. Nothing is preset. Decisions about where everything belongs can be decided together without any precedents already established. It will help make a fresh start for everyone. If there are children, selecting a new home will also help them be excited about the marriage.

Questions

1. Where do you plan to live after you marry?

2. Did either of you live there before? If yes, who?

3. How do you feel about this arrangement? How was the decision made? Do you think this is the best possible choice or is there something else you would prefer?

4. How long do you anticipate living there?

CHAPTER TWO

Finances

*W*hile not the most difficult area in subsequent marriages, like in all marriages, finances are a frequent trouble spot. For some reason, many of us are uncomfortable talking about finances prior to marriage, as though this is just too personal. Therefore, we wait until after the wedding to even discuss the subject of finances in detail. Waiting is not a good idea and will only lead to trouble.

Finances need to be discussed prior to the wedding and definite decisions need to be made about the distribution of funds available to the couple. Of course, these will need to be re-evaluated periodically and adjustments made. However, if the couple has worked out a plan early on, future adjustments will be much easier than if left to chance.

Ron and Julie wanted to get their marriage off on

the right foot. Julie had been married before and had one child, a daughter, who was seven. Ron had not been married before but had lived on his own for twelve years. Each wanted to maintain some financial independence. Therefore, they each kept separate checking and savings accounts. It was not that they did not trust each other. It was more that having separate money that was theirs alone represented a certain autonomy that each treasured.

Julie and Ron sat down prior to the wedding and developed a budget. Each agreed how much of their income would go to household expenses. These they put into a joint account, and they decided to pay the bills together so that each would know just where the money was going. The child support money that Julie received from her former husband would be divided in half – half going into the household account and the other half to be spent on clothing and other needs of Julie's daughter. The money that both Ron and Julie had that did not go into their joint household account was to be kept by each separately for their own use.

For Julie and Ron, this seemed to work well. Not every couple would like such a financial arrangement, however. Some couples want all their money to be put into a common pot representative of their unity as a family. In a subsequent marriage, there is no singular right and wrong way. Each couple must decide what works for them. Some people (both men and women) are reluctant to simply meld their incomes together in a common account from which all bills are paid. Others are only too happy to do so and feel this is as it should be. Each couple needs to talk about what will work best for them.

If there are child support payments being paid or received, these must be talked about prior to the wedding so that there is a good understanding concerning how these will be handled. Similarly, if one or both partners enter the marriage with prior debts or assets, these need to be discussed. Financial matters not talked about before the wedding are sure to cause problems later.

Questions

1. What monthly income will each of you be bringing into the home?

2. Will there be child support income received? How much? What has been the history of payments received?

3. Make a list of expenses anticipated each month. Be sure to include:

> Church and Other Charities
>
> Housing (Rent or Mortgage, Maintenance, Taxes, Insurance)
>
> Child Support Payments

Alimony

Food and other Household Expenses

Utilities

Automobiles (Payments, Upkeep, Gasoline, Insurance)

Loan Payments

Savings

Clothing

Life and Health Insurance

Entertainment

Other

4. How will each of these items be paid? By whom? From what income?

5. Will there be joint checking and savings accounts, or will each of you maintain separate accounts?

CHAPTER THREE

Prenuptial Agreements and Wills

*S*ubsequent marriages can be very complicated. Nowhere is this truer than in the legal areas concerned with what will happen in the event of a divorce or the death of one of the partners. While couples seldom like to talk about such matters when they are making plans for getting married, nevertheless, in the back of each person's mind there is usually a nagging thought that they need to sit down and consider this topic at some time.

Most couples will never draw up a prenuptial agreement. They might talk about it, but most never do it. Part of the reason for not doing a prenuptial is that many couples do not like to enter a marriage with even the thought that they might subsequently divorce. Prenuptials only apply to divorces, and most couples hate to even contemplate such a thought.

Nevertheless, people who have previously gone through a divorce know the reality that divorce happens even to people who do not expect it or want it. They also often feel strongly that they need to protect tangible assets for their children in the event such a thing should happen in the future. Therefore, some do choose to enter the marriage only after a prenuptial agreement has been made.

One of the good things about a prenuptial agreement is that it requires complete disclosure of all financial assets and liabilities of each of the partners. A prenuptial is generally not considered valid if complete disclosure has not taken place. Interestingly, many couples do not talk about finances at all until after they are married—even as to what each person brings into the marriage.

Janice and George did exactly that. Although each had two children from previous marriages and each worried somewhat over whether their income would be adequate, they simply ignored their nagging doubts and plunged ahead with the marriage.

As it turned out, George had a considerable amount of debt related to the time of his first marriage. His divorce and the time following it had only caused him to accumulate even more debt. Janice on the other hand had been very frugal and by living modestly had managed to remain debt free. Janice worried about debt and did not want any. She knew that George had debts when they married but also knew that he was working toward paying them off.

Money was only one of several issues that plagued their marriage. Parenting styles, former spouses, and the attitude of two of the children also made their marriage very difficult. Consequently, after only two years, George and Janice separated and ultimately divorced.

At that point, something occurred that Janice never anticipated. Bill collectors began hounding her over George's debts. Unwittingly, in marrying George she had taken on responsibility for the debt he brought to the marriage. In this case, a prenuptial agreement that spelled out that George's debt would remain his in the event of another divorce might have helped her.

While most people marrying again will not make or need a prenuptial agreement, everyone needs a will. In situations where there are children from an earlier marriage, such wills can become very complex.

There are many horror stories told by adult children where a biological parent who had married again died and because the will inadequately protected their interest, they were in essence disinherited.

Take the case of Lisa, for example. Lisa's father was devastated following the death of her mother. Therefore, Lisa was delighted a few years later when her father met someone else and married again. Lisa had a good relationship with her stepmother, but her brother did not. For various reasons, Lisa's brother never accepted his father's new relationship and would have nothing to do with them.

Many years later, Lisa's father died. A short time later, her stepmother also died. To Lisa's surprise, her stepmother's entire estate then passed on to her biological children, and Lisa received nothing. Lisa's father had intended for Lisa and her brother to receive his share of the estate but had left everything to his wife. The stepmother was so upset with the stepson, however, that she simply passed all of the estate that was now hers on to her biological children.

A stepfamily will must be carefully drawn to protect everyone involved while at the same time providing for the care of a spouse for as long as he or she lives.

Questions

1. List all your financial assets:

   Houses and Property:

   Checking Accounts:

   Savings Accounts:

   Stocks and Bonds:

   Other:

2. List all your debts.

3. What are your concerns about financial arrangements as you enter this marriage?

4. How do you want your children protected in case something was to happen to this marriage?

The Former Spouse

$\mathcal{A}$ long with children from a previous marriage, people who marry again (unless they are widowed) also have former spouses with whom they must interact frequently or at least occasionally. Even the widowed discover that deceased spouses have an impact on their marriage in some very important ways. The relationship with former spouses is an important ingredient in the blending process.

Since it is often overlooked, let us look at how a deceased spouse might affect a remarriage situation. Consider the marriage of Samantha and Lee. Lee's wife died after a four-year battle with breast cancer, leaving him with three children, ages twelve, nine, and seven. Samantha had not been married before.

Since Samantha lived in an apartment and Lee and his children already had a house, it seemed easiest for

Samantha to move into their house and let the children keep familiar surroundings. Little did she realize that the house was booby-trapped. When Samantha tried to rearrange the furniture in the living room, Lee's oldest daughter was furious. "How can you come in here and change things like this? Mom always kept the room this way!" When Samantha wanted to put up new wallpaper in the kitchen, the same daughter objected, "Mom picked out that wallpaper. You can't change it."

It became obvious to Samantha that the children were still deeply involved in their grieving and it was going to take some time and a lot of patience on her part to help them through it. If she had not been as sensitive as she was, Samantha and Lee could have faced many stormy battles.

When there have been divorces, struggles with former spouses are often the topic of many stepfamily arguments. One thing about former spouses is that most are *bad news.* They either want more money all the time, **or** they never pay what they should. They either neglect the kids, **or** they spoil the children, trying to buy their love. Former spouses almost never understand, are manipulative, are immoral, and are financially irresponsible. (Of course, these same former spouses think the same things about *their* former spouses.) Which, or course, is what makes them "ex's"—they could not get along together as marrieds.

Most divorced couples (with children from that marriage) soon learn that divorce does not end the relationship; it simply changes the arena. They must continue to interact periodically throughout their lives. If there are younger children involved, that will mean having to work together with the former spouse in parenting, whether one likes it or not. Being a good parent frequently means putting the interest of the child before one's own. While this should never mean giving the child something he or she should not have (out of guilt or imply because the other parent wants it), it *does* mean being willing to interact with the other parent even though that may be painful.

Such interaction does not mean capitulation or manipulation. The marriage is over and should be put to rest. While this is certainly never easy, it should always remain the goal. The better working relationship you have with your former spouse, the better off your children will be, and the better off your subsequent marriage will be. A strained relationship with a former spouse will only cause emotional friction that rubs off onto all other relationships as well.

Ray seemed to always be fighting with his former wife, Melissa. He was still bitter about his divorce, feeling that his former wife received more in the settlement than was fair. Also, she seemed totally uncooperative when it came to his times of visitation. At the last minute, Melissa would frequently call and say that his daughter had been invited to a birthday party or something else and couldn't come that weekend. Or Ray would arrive at the house only to find no one home. One time he waited over an hour before they showed up.

When Ray married Becky the fighting with Melissa continued. While it might seem that the animosity was only between Ray and Melissa, in actuality, the struggle now involved Becky as well and affected the new marriage as strongly as it had previously affected Ray's life. Ray and Becky found themselves constantly upset over something Melissa did.

It would take Ray and Becky a long time to learn how to be proactive in dealing with Melissa. The stepfamily support group they attended helped a lot. Together they strategized what Ray and Becky could do whenever Melissa tried to sabotage their plans. While not all of these plans worked perfectly, simply realizing that they were not powerless over the situation helped considerably.

The biggest thing that Ray and Becky learned was that their new marriage was primary. While Ray did have to cooperate with his former wife, Melissa, in raising his daughter, whatever Ray and Melissa did affected Becky also. Ray and Becky needed to learn how to interact with Melissa and Ray's daughter in a way that worked for everyone. It was a difficult task that took years to figure out.

Sometimes in subsequent marriages, there will be various relatives that have a continuing relationship with the former spouse. If these relationships are strong and good, they may pose some problems for the remarried couple. Even in cases where there has been a death, some relatives may be less than happy about a subsequent marriage because of their feelings for the deceased.

Relatives frequently do not wish to give up relationships simply because someone has divorced or married again. Nor should they have to. On the other hand, relatives should not be allowed to interfere with the subsequent marriage out of their desire to be supportive to this other person.

Most of the time, such situations are not extremely difficult to solve, but they can be irritating, and unless they are addressed forthrightly, they can pose lasting problems. Without anticipating such problems (or trying to resolve something imaginary) a couple needs to be ready to confront any relative creating a problem in as loving a way as possible and share what is happening.

For example, Henry's mother remained close to his former wife, Beverly, following their divorce. As far as Henry was concerned, that was fine. He neither encouraged nor discouraged them from doing so. After all, it was his divorce, not his mother's.

When Henry married again some five years later,

however, his mother's relationship with his former wife caused some problems because she insisted upon talking about it with his new wife. Since Henry and his mother lived in different states, she would come to visit occasionally and stay for about a week. During that time, Henry's present wife, Rachel, would entertain Henry's mother and take her places, as she believed a good daughter-in-law should. One day, after they were returning from a day of shopping, Henry's mother turned to Rachel and said, "You know, I miss Beverly so much."

Rachel did not know what to say; therefore, at the time she said nothing. When she related the story to Henry, however, he was furious. That night he had a talk with his mother. He told her, "Mom, I think it is great that you and Beverly continue to see each other. I've never tried to stop you. However, I must insist that you not talk about Beverly to Rachel. It is awkward for her and makes her feel that you don't like her as well as you do Beverly. I know you didn't mean to hurt her today, but you did." Henry's mom never brought up the subject of Beverly again.

When there has been a death, the deceased spouse's parents can sometimes cause difficulties when they try to have a relationship with their biological grandchildren while ignoring stepgrandchildren. Children are frequently hurt when some children receive favored treatment. While it is normal for grandparents to have a stronger emotional attachment with their biological grandchildren, with a little coaching, most of the time they can learn to include all the children so as to not create a problem.

Questions

1. Describe in detail your divorce or the circumstances of the death of your mate. (If this is a first marriage for you but you are marrying someone who has been married before, write what you presently know of that event in the life of your partner.)

2. What are your present feelings toward this person?

3. (If Divorced) Describe the working relationship you have with your former spouse as far as raising the children is concerned. In what ways does your former spouse still try to manipulate you? How does this make you feel? What do you do about it?

4. (If Widowed) Describe your grief pilgrimage. How far along do you think you are? What lessons have you learned? In what ways might your former spouse impact your new marriage? How comfortable is your new partner with your previous marriage?

5. Which relatives and friends still have a close relationship with your former spouse? If your spouse is

deceased, which relatives and friends were closest to your spouse?

6. Are any of these people likely to have difficulty with your getting married again?

CHAPTER FIVE

Holidays

*P*robably no time of the year has more hidden landmines for the stepfamily than various holidays, especially the Christmas season. Unless holidays are talked about and planned for very carefully, most families seeking to blend traditions will find the first several holiday seasons less than enjoyable, and some holidays will be simply horrible.

Maggie and Jim had five children between them. Jim's three children came to live with them every Wednesday night and three weekends a month. Maggie's children lived with them all the time except during the summer and some holidays when the children went to live with their father in a distant state.

Maggie and Jim married in August. As they made plans for Thanksgiving that year, the complications of children living in several different families became apparent. On this year, Jim would have his three children from noon on Thanksgiving and through that weekend. Maggie's children would be flying to Colorado on Wednesday that week to go skiing with their dad.

Maggie wanted an old-fashioned Thanksgiving with all of the children present and with Maggie's parents and Jim's parents coming over for dinner. With her children being away on Thanksgiving Day, Maggie tried to set it up so that the family could celebrate Thanksgiving on the Sunday before her children left. There was only one problem. That was the weekend that Jim's former wife was supposed to have their children, and she was unwilling to change her plans. After much agonizing over finding a date when everyone could be there, Maggie and Jim's first Thanksgiving together was finally scheduled for a Sunday two weeks prior to the real Thanksgiving Day. While this was not what Maggie or anyone wanted, it seemed to be the best they could do.

Maggie planned for a wonderful feast. She would bake a turkey with the traditional chestnut stuffing that her mother had taught her to make. Jim's mother was bringing sweet potatoes. Her mother would bring pumpkin and mince meat pies. They would celebrate Thanksgiving as one big happy family.

Sadly, that was not to be the case. Jim's children took one bite of Maggie's chestnut stuffing and said,

"Yech! What *is* this stuff?" "If you don't like it, just don't eat it," Jim told them. Maggie's children refused to even taste Jim's mother's sweet potatoes even though Maggie tried to tell them how good they were. Jim and his kids asked why there weren't any deviled eggs on the table. They always had deviled eggs on Thanksgiving. No one seemed happy with the meal.

After dinner Jim's three children all said, "Are we going to the movies?" In their previous family, going to the movies after Thanksgiving dinner was a tradition. "Not this year," Jim told them. "We decided that we would all stay home and play games." "But we want to go to a movie!" they shouted. "Who wants to play some stupid game?"

Needless to say, Maggie and Jim's first Thanksgiving together was less than what they hoped it would be. Neither of them was prepared for all the difficulties involved, nor were they aware of all the traditions each person harbored about how this holiday should be observed.

The only way to avoid some of these pitfalls is by talking about them beforehand. If Maggie and Jim had sat down with the children prior to planning the event, discussed the menu together (Thanksgiving's menu is filled with traditional foods that vary from family to family), and shared how each person would like to celebrate their first Thanksgiving together, they might have been able to come to some agreement. They certainly would not have walked blindly into the minefield that awaited them.

Christmas gift giving is another minefield through which many in stepfamilies find it difficult to maneuver. In some families, everyone gets a gift for everyone else. These gifts are usually small but they can be very important. In other families, the children get most of the presents, but these may run into the hundreds of dollars. In some homes, Christmas gifts almost cover the floor. In others, there are only a few significant gifts. Unless the family has talked about how they would like to handle Christmas gifts and agreed upon how to merge their different traditions, Christmas can be a difficult time rather than a joyous one.

The same is true concerning birthdays. In some families, birthdays are no big thing. A card, birthday cake, and a small present is all that is expected. In other families, birthdays call for a major celebration. Until the new family has established its own tradition about how birthdays will be celebrated, expectations from the past are likely to create problems.

Each new family seeking to blend traditions would do well to sit down and discuss just how they are going to do it. Even then, coming to agreement will not be easy. Most stepfamilies find that it takes about five years before everyone feels comfortable with holiday traditions.

Questions

1. With a calendar in hand, talk about how your family in the past celebrated each holiday. Concentrate on the big ones but do not skip over any.

2. What expectations are your children going to have concerning the celebration of various holidays?

3. How would you like to blend these traditions? How do you think the children would like this?

4. Set a time to sit down with the children to discuss holiday traditions and how they would like to celebrate them.

Relating to Children From the Previous Marriage

CHAPTER ONE

What Children Experience When a Parent Remarries

*A*lthough many children seem thrilled when a parent announces plans to marry again, what they are usually excited about is a fantasy that this new family will be like their old family. It won't be, and their joy and excitement often turns quickly into displeasure and anger.

Robin and Clark had such an experience. Robin was widowed and Clark was divorced and each had two children. The children had actually brought them together at a ballgame and talked together about their mom and dad getting married. Everything seemed perfect—until the wedding. Suddenly, when everyone finally moved in together, chaos occurred. Robin and Clark sometimes joke that if they had it to do over, they would not have married—just continue to date for the rest of their lives.

What Robin and Clark failed to realize was that the children longed for the fantasy of a nuclear family. Robin's children could not understand that Clark was never going to be like their biological father. Nor could Clark's children appreciate that Robin was not really like their biological mother. None of them understood just how difficult it would be to blend them into a family.

Whether there has been a death or a divorce, children experience grief over the loss of the nuclear family, with mom, dad, and themselves all together. That particular family life has been taken away from them and it hurts. Unless the previous family life of the children involved a lot of pain, children usually desire for a return to their past experience when mom and dad were together. Sometimes, even when the past was not all that good, children still long for a family like they see some of their friends enjoying.

Grief is a long process that usually takes between five and ten years to accomplish. Even then, grief is not something people *get over*. Grief experiences are with them for a lifetime. People do learn to live with such experiences. In time, they adjust. But get over them? Never.

It is often difficult for parents to recognize children's grief at a time when they are excited and happy about a new love. However, what may seem like a joyful experience for the couple about to be married can feel like the end of the world to a child or children. Suddenly Mom or Dad has decided to replace their biological parent with a substitute.

Instinctively, children realize that a parent's remarriage is going to change the relationship they have developed since the divorce or the death of the other parent. Most children and single parents have survived divorce or death by growing very close to each other. When someone dies, or a couple divorces, the parent role changes. For good or bad, children and parents become close friends. They need each other in a way they never did before.

Of course, the parent has another need the children cannot fully appreciate. While parents cling to their children following a death or divorce, adults also long for the love and companionship of another adult in their lives. Finding such a love brings the parent joy. Sharing that joy with children may be difficult, however, for children recognize that the close relationship they had with the parent has suddenly changed. Mom or Dad is spending more time away from them. Dad or Mom doesn't seem to need them as much anymore. When a parent finds another love, children often feel it takes something away from them. Is it any wonder then that what feels like joy to a parent frequently feels like sadness to a child?

In addition, when a parent marries again, that marriage interferes with the common childhood fantasy that mom and dad might get back together again. While children often know that such a thing is unlikely, they usually still hope. One stepmother was talking with a stepdaughter almost twenty years after having married the girl's father, and although they now had a great relationship the girl said, "If I could have anything I wanted in this whole world, it would be to have my mom and dad back together." She told her stepmother that it had nothing to do with her. She simply longed to have her parents together.

Remarriage of a parent interferes with the likelihood of a child's fantasy coming to pass. Another son came to his mother and actually said that he wished that she would marry his father again. Not only had his mother already married again but the boy's father had also. "But what would happen to your father's wife and your stepfather?" she asked the boy. "Oh, they could marry each other," was his reply. In his mind, he had it all figured out.

Many times teenagers are quite hostile to a parent marrying again while the teenager is still in the home. One fifteen-year-old told her mother, "Don't you dare get married before I go away to college." However, this girl's mother had already met a man she wanted to marry. They were even attending our stepfamily support group in anticipation of any difficulties they might encounter. Because of the daughter's words about her mother remarrying, this couple was fearful of telling her about their plans. We strategized together about how they might break the news in the least painful way.

Ultimately, this couple decided to take the daughter out to dinner, feeling that she would be less prone to cause a scene in public. As they were sitting there after dinner, the man began by telling the daughter how much he loved her mother and wanted to marry her. He went on for about five minutes about his feelings for both the mother and the daughter. Finally they told her they had set a date for the wedding. We had cautioned them not to expect a response from the teen because she would probably not be ready to say much. Indeed, her first response was, "Can I go to the bathroom now?"

Being prepared, this couple was very patient with the daughter who quickly came around and is now delighted that they married. Most children need time to adjust. A parent's marriage interrupts the children's lives and certainly changes the relationship they had with the parent before. If a parent is patient and wise, most children will eventually adjust and actually find that the new situation is a blessing rather than a curse. Nevertheless, it will probably take them a while to recognize this.

Questions

1. Describe how each of the children reacted to the death of a parent or the divorce of their parents.

2. Over time, how did everyone adjust to that situation?

3. Describe the attitude of each of the children regarding your plans to marry again.

4. How would you contend with any of the situations described in this chapter?

CHAPTER TWO

Discipline

*M*any people seem to think that discipline is simply punishing children for wrongdoing. While punishment may certainly be a part of discipline, punishment can never be the primary ingredient of discipline. Punishment can only be one possible method in helping children learn how to take charge of themselves. Unless children learn self-discipline, they will never accomplish very much in life.

Discipline is little more than setting goals and achieving them. A wise person once said, "A genius is someone who shoots at a target no one else sees and hits it." However, no one (genius or otherwise) can hit any target without the discipline of performing all the tasks necessary to develop and employ the skills involved.

I once heard someone remark, "I wish I could play

the piano." I replied that I thought they probably could if they were willing to devote about an hour *every day* for several years in practicing the piano. Certainly, natural talent plays a part in any endeavor, but only a small part. The greater challenge in any accomplishment is in exercising the discipline required. Thomas Edison once said that invention was only 1% inspiration and 99% perspiration.

No one is born with self-discipline. It is always learned. Children are born wanting what they want when they want it. In the most part, parents are eager to fulfill the desires of their children. Which is fine in the very early years of a child's life, but not so good as the child continues to grow, for if the child does not learn how to achieve his desires on his own, the parent has not prepared the child very well for life.

A very wise set of parents (in this case a biological father and a stepmother) decided to teach the teenage daughter how to handle her money better. The stepmother became upset that the daughter was always asking her father for money and he was giving it to her. (Stepparents can almost always see problems to which the biological parent is unaware.)

They asked the daughter to sit down and make a list of all the things she needed money for each month, including lunch at school, clothing, entertainment, and anything else. The girl came up with an amount below what the parents expected. They told her that they would give her that amount each month; either in one payment or as many payments as she wanted, but that she could have no more. The daughter was delighted and chose to receive the money in a lump sum at the beginning of the month.

As might be expected, the daughter spent all of the money in the first two weeks. The parents were prepared for this and anticipated giving her an advance on the next month's allowance. To their surprise, the daughter never asked for any more. They were never sure how she made it through the month without additional money, but she did. The next month, the daughter not only made the money last an entire month, she had money left over. She was saving for something big that she wanted. In only two months time, she had begun learning a valuable lesson that would serve her well for the rest of her life.

Discipline is about teaching children how to not only survive on their own but to achieve and accomplish their goals. While most parents would never dream of doing children's homework for them, many parents end up doing just about everything else rather than teaching the children how to do things for themselves. Remember the old proverb, "Give a person a fish and that person will be hungry tomorrow. Teach a person to fish and that person will never be hungry again." The same applies to children.

When it comes to who should teach discipline to

children in a stepfamily, there are two schools of thought. One way of looking at this issue says that the biological parent is the person who takes on the task of discipline because children are not ready in the early years of a stepfamily to accept discipline from a stepparent. The other thought is that both biological and stepparent jointly share in the task of discipline.

Problems with discipline arise when couples do not agree on what discipline the children need. Stepparents can always see flaws in the children that are not at all clear to the biological parent. Biological parents tend to defend their children no matter what. It is almost instinctive. Also, most biological parents have fallen into a "friendship" relationship with their children during single parenting simply as a survival technique. While the parent may be ready to move back to "parenting," the children seldom are. Children like the freedom and camaraderie they have developed with the biological parent and do not want to give it up.

While many biological parents are ready for some help in raising the children, they expect the stepparent to do it "their" way. That almost never happens. People simply have different ideas about how children should behave. Therefore, it is important that every couple discuss parenting styles and come to an understanding about how they can help these children become well adjusted and strong adults. It is less important who teaches discipline to children than it is that the couple develops agreement about that discipline. Such agreement does not come easily. It must be worked at through many discussions.

If children become aware that the biological parent and the stepparent disagree over the issue of discipline, the children will almost always use that disagreement to cause a rift in the marriage. Many children consider it a victory if the stepparent leaves, and discipline is the area where most disagreements develop. The wise stepfamily couple will present a united front to the children. Such unity is to everyone's advantage.

Questions

1. How do your parenting styles differ? On what issues do you agree? On what issues do you disagree?

2. What are some problems the stepparent-to-be sees in how the children behave? Where does the biological parent agree and disagree with this assessment?

3. Regarding the idea presented in this chapter that discipline should be about helping children become independent adults, how can the two of you work together to help the children develop the skills necessary to live on their own?

CHAPTER THREE

Younger Children

$\mathcal{I}$t would seem that younger children (under age ten) are the easiest to blend into a new family. Certainly this is true in most families. However, I am uncomfortable with the thought that simply because younger children present fewer problems, they adjust more easily than older children do. It could well be that younger children do not have the communication skills or the power to cause many of the problems that older children pose.

We do know that younger children are likely to feel responsible for either the divorce or the death of a parent that precedes remarriage. In fact younger children often refer to a divorce as "my divorce" rather than the divorce of their parents. Divorce is very personal to children. In a similar way when a parent marries again, younger children are likely to talk about getting married themselves.

Tommy was only three when his parents divorced. He could not understand what he had done to cause his mother to leave, but he was sure that she did not love him anymore. Even though she told him that she certainly did love him, Tommy did not believe it. If she loved him, she would not have left.

It had not been an easy decision for Tommy's mother to grant custody to her husband, but at the time it seemed to be the only practical solution. Her job required extensive travel, and she knew that Tommy would have a more stable life with his father than with her. Nevertheless, to Tommy, his mother's leaving meant that she did not love him anymore, and he must have done something to cause her not to love him.

To young children, the world revolves around them. They see themselves as the center of the universe. When children are born, they are unable to even distinguish boundaries between themselves and other people. Parents are simply extensions of themselves that they learn to control in the same way that they control their hands and their feet. It should not surprise us then that young children feel responsible for either a divorce or a death, because they see themselves as being responsible for everything that happens. They may not understand what happened, but they usually feel responsible.

Wise parents, therefore, tell younger children over and over that the divorce or the death of a parent was not their doing. Telling children once never works. They need to be told time and again that they were not responsible for the death or the divorce. They need to be told repeatedly what will happen to them and be reassured of their parent's love.

Two years after the divorce, Tommy's father married again. When his father started dating Diane, Tommy was thrilled. Now, he could have the home and family that he missed so much. From the beginning, Tommy was asking his father and Diane when they were going to get married. When they finally told Tommy that he was going to be in the wedding, Tommy told his friends that "he" was getting married. Tommy longed for his family to be like that of his friend, John, whose parents were together. Now, it seemed like that was going to happen.

Tommy was trying to put his world back together again. It seemed to have broken apart when his parents separated, but now he would have a new family and everything would be OK. Now he could be normal again—just like his friend, John.

Of course, all of this was a fantasy that was sure to break down. Fantasies always give way to reality over time. Diane was never going to replace Tommy's mother. She was different, as all people are different. Also, Diane had never had children before and she had not yet learned what works and does not work when trying to raise children.

She did not understand at first that it is normal for

a six-year-old child to simply ignore a parent's request to pick up the toys and get ready for dinner. When Tommy continued playing, Diane felt that he did not respect her authority, even though Tommy would have done the same thing had she been his biological mother. It was going to take several years for Diane to discover what raising a child was really like. It was also going to take time for Tommy to start loving Diane for what she really was like instead of the fantasy he had imagined she would fulfill.

Younger children do blend into a new family more quickly than older children do. They are more open to accepting the authority of another adult. They do not see themselves as having the power to resist. However, younger children often rebel in subtle ways that can drive stepparents nuts.

Tommy was upset that he did not have his father to himself anymore. It seemed that they never did any-thing alone—without Diane. "Why does she have to go everywhere we do?" he complained to his friends. She was nice *sometimes* but he missed those times alone with his dad. And why was she so bossy? His dad never yelled at him when he didn't pick up his toys right away.

Without ever planning it, Tommy just started doing things that needled Diane. He found that if he came into the room and walked past her to talk to his dad, she became upset. If he kept his hat on when he came to dinner, she always made him take it off, but he heard his dad say to her later on, "Don't be so rough on the boy." Therefore, Tommy often came to dinner with his hat on. Tommy quickly learned hundreds of ways to get his dad and Diane to argue *about him*.

Blended family couples with younger children must present a united front, for children will take advantage of any breach they find. While this is difficult for most biological parents, it is vitally important that the biological parent tell the children from the beginning that the stepparent has complete authority in the house. Then the biological parent needs to back it up. Anything less will put the children in a position of power. If the biological parent and stepparent disagree, they must discuss those differences at a time and place when the children are not present. Telling the children that the stepparent is here to stay and that they might as well get used to it will also help the children adjust and move on.

Questions

1. List the names and ages of all the children under the age of ten. Beside each name write down how each has responded to the idea of your marriage.

2. What behaviors (if any) have you observed that

indicate the child (children) might be less than happy about the upcoming wedding?

3. How are you planning to include the children in the wedding?

4. How will you establish the stepparent's authority for the children?

CHAPTER FOUR

Teenagers

*Y*outh from ages ten to twenty create the most problems for stepfamilies. That shouldn't surprise anyone, because this age group creates the most difficulties for nuclear families as well. The teen years are simply a rough time. Growing up and becoming independent is hard for both teenagers and their parents. Add to that struggle someone not biologically bonded to the teen that nevertheless has some authority over the youth in question and the difficulty is compounded considerably.

Brian and Cynthia were both teenagers when their mother married again. Brian had just turned seventeen and his sister, Cynthia, was two months shy of becoming fourteen. To say that they were less than delighted with their mother's decision to marry would be an understatement. Both of them were angry. "Why couldn't you have at least waited until we left home?" Brian said. While Cynthia was less adamant about it, her mother's marriage was an irritant she would have preferred to do without. Both children had just begun to adjust to their parents' divorce some three years earlier, and now they had to deal with a stepparent.

While many people expect teenagers to have some consideration for the happiness of their parents, when it comes to remarriage it is important to keep in mind that just as the world of children revolves almost completely around themselves, the same is generally true about teenagers. As far as most youth are concerned, how this marriage affects them will be of primary importance. Certainly, most teens will care if mom or dad is happy, but for most youth, their own world and what is important to them will always be paramount.

When Brian's mother remarried, Brian decided to basically ignore the situation. He planned to leave home after graduation in another year anyway. Choosing a college in another state simply took on a new importance. He was not about to let his mother mess up his life. If he couldn't get into a college he liked, he would join the Navy. No way was he going to live with them any longer than he had to.

After his mother married Raymond, Brian tried to simply stay out of sight. He retreated to his room as often as possible. Raymond, however, was somewhat pushy and constantly asked Brian to do things that his mother had never expected him to do before—like mow the yard and take out the garbage. While Brian resented Raymond's authority, to keep peace Brian usually went along. Most of the time, Brian stayed busy at school.

Cynthia rather liked Raymond and enjoyed having a man around again. Cynthia had been devastated when her father left and she missed him terribly. She had seen her father only three times in the three years since the divorce and felt very hurt that he did not seem to love her anymore.

Raymond did seem to care, but Cynthia was well aware of Brian's anger, and she wondered if she shouldn't be angrier as well. Everything had seemed to be settling down after the divorce. They had survived as a single-parent family. Then her mother started dating Raymond. Cynthia was confused. She did not know what she should feel.

When dealing with teenagers in stepfamilies, it is important to keep in mind the purpose of the teen years. Stepfamilies that are formed during these years are somewhat at contrary purposes with the natural development of children. Children are seeking to pull away from the family during the teen years. They are trying to become independent. Certainly, independence is what good parents want for their children. However, getting there can be very painful.

When a stepfamily is formed, both the biological parent and the stepparent naturally want the family to grow close and everyone within the family to learn to love and respect each other. However, the couple wants closeness to develop at the very time teenagers are trying to pull away. During the teen years, children are seeking to become autonomous. Family closeness is not likely to be one of *their* goals. The teen agenda revolves around leaving the home rather than strengthening the home, and no matter how hard parents try to fight it, the natural process of growing up and becoming independent will almost always win out. What loving parents would want their children not to mature and live on their own?

Therefore, the best thing both biological parents and stepparents can do is help the teenager complete the process of becoming independent within safe boundaries. Teenagers are not mature. Their judgment is limited. They need guidance. However, the goal is always to help them develop independence.

The rules throughout the teen years must allow more and more leeway for teenagers to test out their judgment. Remember that it will not be many more years before those teens will be entirely on their own. Also, bear in mind that in this process, teenagers will make mistakes. Maturity only comes with experience, and the experience of learning from our mistakes is one of the ways all of us learn best. Therefore, both biological parent and stepparent must be careful to use mistakes in judgment made by teenagers as a learning tool—not a reason to punish. Punishment usually has little effect upon teenagers.

That does not mean taking away consequences. All wrong action has consequences. These can be very helpful learning tools if they are consistent and if the teenager feels loved in the process.

As part of the learning process, teens need to be involved in dealing with the consequences of mistakes in judgment. For parents and stepparents to simply "lay down the law" will usually only make the teenager more defensive and stubborn. Asking the teen what needs to be done will force that teen to look at the situation. Involving the teen in the solution also helps the teenager to learn.

One weekend, Brian, the seventeen-year-old in the story above, had gone to a party that got out of hand and where the police had been called. Brian's mother and stepfather were called to come and get him. Needless to say, they were very upset.

"I thought you told us that John's parents were going to be home while this party was going on" said Raymond, Brian's stepfather.

"That's what John told me," replied Brian.

"When did you discover they weren't home?" asked his mother.

"When I got there," said Brian.

"The police said there was a lot of drinking going on," Brian's stepfather said, more as a question about what Brian knew than as a statement.

"That goes on at a lot of parties," said Brian.

Brian's mother wanted to ask if Brian had been drinking, but she knew that he would probably just become defensive if she did. Therefore, she asked him, "Brian, how can we avoid something like this ever happening again?"

"I don't know," Brian replied.

"Well, I don't want you to answer right now, anyway," his mother said. "What I want you to do is think about it and come up with a plan whereby you will never be at a party again where alcohol or drugs are being used or where the parents are not home. When you have come up with your plan, I want you to write it down and give it to us. Then we will talk about it and see. Do you understand?"

Happy to be off the hook, Brian quickly agreed and went to his room. The next day, Brian worked on the plan for a little while but could not come up with anything he really liked, so he put it aside. Since neither his mother nor his stepfather said anything more, Brian didn't either. Friday night, Brian told his mother that he planned to stop at Peter's house after the football game.

"I'm afraid you can't go to the game tonight, Brian," said his mother.

"Why not?" asked Brian incredulously.

"You still haven't come up with the plan we talked about the other night. Until you do, there will be no going out except to school."

"That's not fair!" yelled Brian.

"Well I don't like it either," said his mother. "Raymond and I had plans for tonight, but we're staying home. Until you figure out a way where we all will know that we won't have to go through another night like the one last week, I guess we all are grounded."

Brian was furious. He thought that his mother and stepfather had forgotten about the whole thing. When they really did stay home that night, Brian decided that he might as well work on a plan. He knew that he could not get away with simply saying that he would just not go to any parties where there was going to be alcohol or drugs. Therefore, he put in his plan that he would not go to any party where the parents were not going to be present and he would even let his mother know the names of the parents so that she could check. (Although he hoped she wouldn't, Brian knew she would.) He also put in his plan that if he ever saw anyone at a party doing drugs or drinking alcohol, that he would leave.

When they were sitting in the living room reading Brian's plan, Raymond said, "It looks good Brian. I commend you for a good plan. Only one thing remains. What should happen if you don't do these things?"

"I don't know," said Brian. "You guys have to figure that out."

"No," replied Brian's mother. "You do. That has to be part of the plan," and she handed it back to Brian.

Within a short time, Brian was back. He agreed that if he broke the plan that he would lose all driving privileges for a month. Knowing how important Brian's car was to him, his mother and stepfather accepted the plan.

What Brian's mother and stepfather had done was help him learn from his mistake. By making him come up with a plan kept them from being the "bad guys." Also, by staying home themselves and being "grounded" along with him showed a lot of love. This incident was a turning point in this stepfamily's development.

One more point needs to be made when talking about teenagers in stepfamilies. Many teens do not want to involve themselves emotionally with a stepparent because they do not trust that the marriage will last. They have been hurt before, either through the divorce of their parents or even through a death. They do not want to be hurt again. Sometimes it takes several years before these teens begin to trust again. About the only thing parents can do is continue to show the teen that this commitment is for life. On the other hand, if the teenagers hear a lot of quarreling, their doubt will be reinforced.

Teenagers are difficult, but these years are very important in their development. Good stepfamilies give them a safe environment in which to grow.

Questions

1. List the names of all children between the ages of ten and twenty that either partner has. What was the reaction of each when told that you were getting married?

2. What differences do you have in styles of discipline? How do you plan to resolve these differences?

3. Strategize how you can help each of the children become independent during their teen years.

CHAPTER FIVE

Adult Children

*M*any couples mistakenly believe that because children are grown and on their own, they will not impact the marriage. Generally, adult children do have the least impact upon a stepfamily. However, to think that they will cause no problems is naïve. Some adult children have been known to be downright destructive. Almost all have some adjusting to do.

Keep in mind that one partner has a bond and history with those children not shared by the other partner. In a similar way, the children have a bond and history with only half of the marrying couple. Also, the adult children are aware that marriage will change their relationship with the parent. It has to. Following the parent marrying again, adult children simply cannot relate to that parent independently anymore. The new husband or wife must always be considered.

Carol was delighted when her mother started dating Fred. Her mother and father had been divorced for six years. While her father had remarried, Carol worried about her mother. Her mother lived in another city about a three-hour drive away and while they talked on the phone almost every day, it still troubled Carol that her mother was alone.

Carol and her mother had always been close. Carol was thirty-five and had two children, ages six and three. When Carol's husband took a job in another city and they moved away, it had been an adjustment for both Carol and her mother. Whenever Carol's mother came to visit, they would stay up most of the night talking. Carol was simply not prepared for how that was going to change.

Not only did the visits occur less frequently, when Carol's mother did visit, Fred was along. It wasn't that Carol disliked Fred. She simply missed those times alone with her mother. And in many ways, Fred was a stranger. It would be several years before Fred felt like part of the family.

Whenever a parent marries again, all children of all ages must make a major emotional adjustment in their relationship with both the parent and the new stepparent. However, when the children are adults themselves, the term stepparent will seldom apply and adult children will usually view this new person as simply the husband or wife of their mother or father.

Occasionally adult children worry about what will happen to their inheritance if mom or dad marries again. While this may seem mercenary, nevertheless worries about what will happen when mom or dad dies can be an irritant that affects the current relationship with adult children.

Talking with adult children prior to the marriage about inheritance issues often helps. Ignoring the issue only lets it fester. Some couples choose to take out insurance policies on the parent made out to the children to cover inheritance matters. Others find similar creative ways to insure that children from a previous marriage will at least receive something when a biological parent dies to show that the children still matter. Inheritance is about more than money. Various pieces of furniture, dishes, jewelry, and other items that are remembered from the past often are even more important than financial considerations.

The horror stories I hear regarding inheritance are always from children whose surviving parent remarries and subsequently leaves everything to a new spouse. Most of the time, these children do not care so much that they did not receive a lot of money. They are hurt that they were not considered as important as the new spouse's children who ended up with everything. They usually say, "It just wasn't fair."

Questions

1. What has been the attitude of each of the adult children upon hearing of your coming marriage?

2. Have you talked with adult children about how your marriage will change your relationship? What are some things you will still be able to do? What are some others that are not likely to happen any more?

3. Have you talked about inheritance issues in regard to the children each of you has from a previous marriage? How will you insure that each of the children will receive something when you die?

The Wedding and Support Thereafter

CHAPTER ONE

Avoiding Mistakes

From experience I have learned that some wedding plans that might seem appropriate, and even preferable, are, in fact, mistakes to be avoided if at all possible. Three of these mistakes that people who have children from a previous marriage sometimes make are: 1.) eloping, 2.) not telling friends about the marriage until after the wedding, and 3.) not getting adequate pre-marital counseling.

Eloping

There is a real temptation for people who have been married before to try to avoid the hassle of a wedding. Weddings can be a time of stress. Wanting to escape all the stress is understandable. However, couples who elope and tell children and family that they are married after the fact, generally find a lot of hard feelings that may well take months if not years to heal.

Kevin and Patricia were such a couple. Both had been married before and they had three children between them—Patricia with two and Kevin with one. One weekend when the children were all with the former spouses, Patricia and Kevin simply went out of state and got married.

"Guess what we did?" they asked their children when everyone was together again.

"What?" the youngest asked.

"We got married on Saturday," Patricia answered.

Contrary to what Kevin and Patricia expected, none of the children seemed excited even through they had been asking them for some time when they were going to get married. Kevin's daughter said that she had to go somewhere and disappeared. Patricia and Kevin just looked at each other and wondered what had happened.

What this couple failed to understand was that children (especially younger children) often think of a parent's wedding as something that happens to them. Small children frequently say something like, "I'm getting married this Saturday." Even older children understand that the marriage of a parent affects them considerably. For a parent to tell the children after the fact gives the children no time at all to react to the news either positively or negatively prior to the event. Also, many children want to be there when a parent marries. They see themselves in the event. Eloping robs them of the possibility.

Not Telling Friends About the Marriage Until After the Wedding

A similar mistake occurs when a couple gets married with family present but where friends have not been told prior to the wedding. Again, this seems to be so simple and certainly a way to avoid the hassles of a large wedding.

I came to recognize this as a mistake after one couple in our singles group did exactly what I am talking about. They decided to have a small family wedding in the chapel and then later that evening show up at a dance the singles were having, announcing that they were now married. They asked me to keep it a secret because they wanted to surprise everyone.

Now, all the singles in the group knew that this couple was going to get married. That certainly was not a secret. However, no one knew when. The biggest surprise was how people reacted. The singles were not pleasantly surprised and supportive. Instead, they were angry and upset. The singles had known this couple for several years and considered themselves part of their family. Not to be told until after the event hurt. It took many months to repair some of these relationships.

Not Getting Adequate Pre-Marital Counseling

Many people marrying again do not feel the need for much pre-marital counseling. They have been married before and feel that they already have a good understanding of what marriage is all about. While I do believe that previous marital experience is a benefit, stepfamilies are so complicated that previous nuclear family experience is of minimal value. People marrying again can use all the help they can get.

What is adequate in terms of pre-marital counseling? Since you are reading this book, you have already made a good start. Reading at least one book about stepfamilies is very important. Reading more than one is helpful.

Another important ingredient in pre-marital counseling is a good pre-marital inventory administered by a trained counselor, either a pastor or other professional. The pre-marital inventory will help couples recognize issues in their relationship that need attention very quickly. Then they can make plans to address those issues with someone who can help. Every relationship can be improved.

Questions

1. Discuss your wedding plans in light of the mistakes listed above.

CHAPTER TWO

Involving Children in the Wedding

*N*ot all children want to be involved in a parent's wedding. However, all children want the parents to care about them. Therefore, children should always be *invited* to participate in the wedding in some particular way. While forcing a child or children to be involved would probably create barriers that might take years to overcome, inviting the children to participate will let them know that they are wanted there.

Younger children will generally want to participate. As mentioned earlier, younger children often think of the wedding of a parent as *their* wedding. They see themselves very much involved.

Teenagers and adult children may have mixed ideas about being involved in a parent's wedding. Nevertheless, they should be invited to participate. While some will decline, most will want to be involved, and all will appreciate the offer. Not to be invited to participate in such an event is almost like saying, "We don't care about you."

Children of all ages can participate in a parent's wedding in a variety of ways. In most cases, having the children stand with the parent during the ceremony is very appropriate. I like to even include children in the words that I use.

Usually after talking with the couple about what marriage should be, I say something like: "Both of you (or whatever is appropriate) enter this marriage with children (and then I say the names of the children). The commitment you make here is not only a commitment to each other but a commitment to each of these children as well. It is only with patience, effort and a lot of love that this family is going to become what you desire.

"To the children, let me say that this marriage will have an affect upon you as well. It can be a wonderful opportunity for you to gain another important adult person in your life with whom to share many things. This will not just happen, however. Everyone involved must work at it. But you are part of this family, and I urge you to commit yourselves to this family as (Names) commit themselves to each other and to you, and may the Lord God bless you all."

If the children are older, I usually say, "Even though

these children are now adults themselves, they remain your children. That will never change and it certainly will have an impact upon your marriage, because one of you already has a close bond that will take years for the other to develop."

To adult children I say, "Even though you are now adults yourselves, this marriage certainly affects you, because from now on you must relate to both your (mother or father—whichever is appropriate) and (his/her) new spouse, whereas before you related only to your parent. That changes things, and some of those changes are not easily made. I urge you to support this marriage on behalf of your (mother/father), and may God bless you all."

I have only encountered a few children who did not appreciate being involved in their parent's wedding. These are usually easily known by the scowls on their faces. However, even they seem to adjust more quickly because the parent made the effort to involve them from the beginning.

Some couples like to include a symbolic act during the ceremony to signify the creation of a new family. One couple had each family member put a flower in a vase creating a very nice bouquet. Another couple gave small gifts to each of the children while they were giving rings to each other. They also spoke to the children of how they wanted them to be a part of the family. There are many ways to involve the children.

Questions

1. How do you plan to involve the children in your wedding? What has been their reaction to these plans?

2. Will the minister address the children during the ceremony? What would you like the minister to say?

3. Are any of the children likely to create a problem during the wedding? Strategize how you plan to deal with any disturbance.

CHAPTER THREE

Joining a Stepfamily Support Group

O ne of the best insurance policies you can take out for a successful blending of your family will be to become involved in a stepfamily support group. Without help, only 40% of all people who marry with children from a previous marriage stay together. Those are not very good odds. With the help of a support group those figures can change in your favor, because 80% of families in a stepfamily support group succeed. With this one simple act you can double your odds of staying together.

What happens in a support group that makes such a difference? I will never forget the stepfamily seminar that Betty and I attended at Georgia State University. It was only one day, but it changed the way we both understood our situation. Prior to that time both of us felt locked into a marriage without much hope. The other person simply would not make the adjustments necessary to make our new family succeed. Each of us believed that we were right in our actions.

Betty thought that I was terribly insensitive about how much of an outsider she felt in her own home when my daughter was around. My daughter and I would make plans and then invite Betty to join us. We would sit and talk about times when Betty was not around. In my excitement over being with my daughter, I was unable to comprehend what Betty was trying to tell me.

For my part, I believed that Betty was simply not being very caring about my relationship with my daughter. We did not get that many opportunities to see each other. Why couldn't Betty give me my time with Kim, and then Betty and I would have our time together? Betty was simply demanding too much.

Attending the seminar at Georgia State really made a difference in our lives. At the time we went there, neither of us was sure that our marriage could survive. Just listening to the presenters and other people like us share their stories quickly showed us that we were not alone. I remember turning to Betty and saying, "It's not us. It's the situation."

That simple realization changed everything. Suddenly, we had a problem we could work on together. It was not a matter of one of us needing to change. Together, we needed to both understand the truth about stepfamilies and develop techniques that would allow everyone within the family to feel at home. The struggles that we had been experiencing were as normal as breathing. Knowing that allowed us to relax and begin the work we needed to do.

Realizing that stepfamilies were different, Betty and I decided that there had to be other people in similar circumstances at our church in Roswell, Georgia. We contacted four other couples and met together one night at a local restaurant. What a night! We could not stop talking. In fact, we closed the restaurant that evening. Then we started meeting regularly, first as a planning team designing our Stepfamily Ministry and then twice a month as a support group. I even asked that my title at the church be changed from Minister of Singles to Minister of Singles *and* Stepfamilies.

Over the years, hundreds of couples have come through that support group. Many times I heard someone say, "Without this group, we would not still be married." Betty and I agree. The stepfamily support group kept us going on several occasions.

How can you go about finding a stepfamily support group? You might begin by contacting several churches in your area to see if they have such a ministry. If they do, try them out. Not all groups are the same, however, and any particular group may or may not meet your needs. You will know rather quickly if a group is for you. If you find it helpful, keep going. Attend even when everything is going well in your family life. You may be able to help others. If you discover a group that simply wants to feel sorry for themselves and does not seek for solutions to the problems raised, try another group.

If after trying you still have been unable to find a stepfamily support group, then perhaps God is calling upon you to start one. If you think, "We're not qualified to do such a thing," remember—God does not call the qualified, God qualifies the called. Betty and I were certainly not the least bit qualified when we began our Stepfamily Ministry. We were experiencing very serious marital problems. Do not let a lack of qualification stop you from meeting with other stepfamily couples for support. I would suggest you contact your own church and ask for assistance. Most churches will be delighted for the opportunity.

Questions

1. Is there a stepfamily support group that meets in your area? When do they meet?

2. Can you attend their meetings prior to your wedding? Call and find out.

3. If there are no groups meeting in your area, ask your pastor for the names of other recently married stepfamilies that might be willing to help you develop a group.

CHAPTER FOUR

Agreeing to Counseling Whenever Needed

*T*here is no better time to agree to go to a counselor whenever needed than right now, before you get married. I ask every couple I marry to make a commitment to each other that they will agree to counseling at any time during their marriage that the *other* person believes it would be appropriate. Seldom during a time of conflict will both persons think that counseling is needed. By making a commitment prior to the beginning of such a conflict, it will be easier to follow through.

Betty and I have found counseling to be beneficial several times in our marriage. Most of these times occurred even after we were in the stepfamily support group. These were times when we had come to an impasse that neither of us could see a way through. Usually, we had been arguing over something for several days or months before coming to the decision that we needed help. It is truly amazing how stubborn all of us can be at times. However, in all those times that we sought help with our problems, the most sessions we ever had with a counselor were two. Most of the times, we found no need to continue counseling after one session. We had found a way out of the struggle.

I find it truly amazing how often I have found this to be true, not only in our lives but in the lives of others with whom I have worked. Counseling need not be an ongoing process, especially if the couple has a support group with whom to share. Counseling is simply allowing an independent outside person help identify the real issues of a problem and discover solutions that a couple was unable to see before.

What is it about counseling that so many people find difficult to accept? First, to enter counseling, a person has to admit there is a problem. While most of the time the fact that a problem exists should be readily apparent, most people are pretty good at denial. Some are extremely reluctant to face problems because conflict is very scary to them. Conflict, especially conflict that the couple cannot resolve by themselves, may indicate that the marriage is in trouble and could end. Therefore, some people would rather pretend that the conflict does not exist. While such pretense does not make the conflict disappear, for these people it seems less frightening than facing it squarely.

A second reason that people sometimes avoid counseling is that counseling means that they must share their thoughts and feelings with someone else. Sharing is very difficult for some people. It also means that the counselor could find someone's ideas and behaviors to be bad or wrong. While experience tells me that this seldom occurs with a trained counselor, nevertheless, that is a fear that many have. Going to counseling means testing out one's position and seeking change, something that many are reluctant to do.

Prior to marriage, most couples cannot believe they will ever have any serious problems in their marriage. I assure all couples that they will. Living with another person different from oneself is difficult. None of us thinks the same. None of us has the same comfort level with how a home is kept. None of us has the same ideas about raising children or responding to children's needs.

When we fall in love, we actually fall in love with a fantasy. We fall in love with a fantasy of what life will be like with this person. But fantasies are illusions, and like all illusions they fade in the light of reality. In time, all people find that they must live with a person as he or she really is, not the person they imagined them to be. Learning to love that real person (and his or her children) is what marriage is all about. Counseling can often help.

Questions

1. Do each of you agree to counseling at any time in your marriage that your partner thinks it will be beneficial?

2. Where might you find a counselor that you could see?

CHAPTER FIVE

A Blending of Faiths

hile this book has been primarily concerned with the interpersonal relationships of husband, wife, and children in stepfamilies, there is another dimension that can easily make the difference in determining whether a family succeeds or not. That dimension is faith. Faith is a matter of committing ourselves to God's will rather than our own. Faith is a matter of trusting God to lead us—sometimes through scary places. Faith is a matter of will more than feelings. Therefore, the faith dimension cannot be ignored if a stepfamily is to become all that it can be.

When a couple marries, they create a covenant with each other and with God. They ask God to bless their marriage as they pledge their love and commitment to one another. They invite God to have a primary place in their family. This is a holy time, which is why it often takes place in a church setting. However, whether it occurs in church, home, or some other place is not important. God is everywhere, and the sanctity of the marriage is not fixed to the location.

For the covenant to work, God must be given a primary position in the family. There used to be a saying, "The family that prays together stays together." While that is somewhat cliche, it is true that the attitude of both children and adults changes when God is invited into the relationship. Praying before meals, having family devotions, praying at family meetings, and intentionally asking God to guide the family in daily living really does make a difference. Family members simply cannot pray for each other and act hateful at the same time.

Stepfamilies often include another factor regarding the faith dimension of the family—the blending of faiths. While sometimes all the family members share a common faith background, more often than not there is a faith diversity that must also be blended. It is usually easy enough to make a decision about what church you want to attend if there is only the couple. However, when there are also children who have a history and feelings to contend with, such a decision can become very complicated.

Both Dennis and Myra each had two children from previous marriages. The children had been active in their respective churches throughout most of their lives. Dennis's oldest son was seventeen and even talked about possibly becoming a minister. His other son was fourteen and said that he did not like church at all. However, the thought of changing churches did not seem like an option for either of Dennis's boys. Myra's children, ages ten and seven, while younger than their stepbrothers, certainly did not want to leave their church and their church friends.

Not having worked out this complication prior to the wedding, Myra and Dennis were faced with a dilemma the first weekend the family was all together. Neither Dennis nor Myra wanted to go separate ways to church on their first weekend as a family. At the same time, they did not want to take the children away from their respective churches.

That Saturday, in the midst of a lot of confusion and frustration, they all sat down together to talk over the problem. After laying out the situation, during which the children were quite adamant about not changing, Dennis asked that they take a moment to ask God to help them with their decision.

"Let's begin by each of us silently praying that God will guide us in finding a solution as to which church we will attend," Dennis said. "We may not understand how it is possible to work this out, but God knows." Obediently, they all bowed their heads and prayed.

No brilliant solutions came to Myra, Dennis, and the children that Saturday. God's timetable is seldom as rapid as we want. After much discussion, it was decided that the children could continue to go to their old churches and Dennis and Myra would go to another church of their choice together. It made for a very hectic Sunday, but everyone in the family felt that he or she had a say and had been heard. About four months later, Myra's children decided to go with their mother and stepfather to their church where they discovered several friends from school. Dennis's boys remained at their old church throughout their teen years.

Sometimes, there are no simple solutions to the blending of faiths. What Myra and Dennis discovered was that it was more important to respect the history and feelings of their children than force the family to worship together. As long as the children were active in a church, Dennis and Myra decided they would be satisfied.

Making God the head of one's household enables everyone to seek the common good rather than his or her individual way. Praying together openly conveys this attitude. Stepfamilies need not go it alone. God will help if invited.

Questions

1. What is the faith background of each of the families?

2. If the backgrounds are different, what decisions have been made about how you will express your faith as a family? How do the children feel about that decision?

3. If there is a conflict, how can a solution be found?

Section Five

Leader's Guide for Group Study

Leader's Guide

*T*here are always several ways a book may be studied by a group, ranging all the way from a one-time overview of the book to a detailed, chapter by chapter, in-depth study. If this book is being studied by a group of pastors who might use it in pre-marital counseling, an overview may well be best. If a singles Sunday school class or fellowship group is doing the study, a section-by-section study approach will probably work better than an overview. Some groups may even want to take it slower and consider the workbook chapter by chapter. In this leader's guide only the first two approaches will be considered. A group studying the book chapter by chapter will need to be creative but will benefit from reading over both of the following study suggestions.

A One-Time Overview Study

If copies of *In Love Again & Making It Work* have not been secured for each participant, have several copies available so that persons may see them before and after the meeting.

1. **Get Acquainted**
   a) Divide into small groups of four or five people and ask everyone to share:
   b) Name
   c) One or two things about themselves
   d) Why they are here

2. **A Theology of Remarriage**
   a) Choose two or three ideas from the *Preface: A Theology of Remarriage* to highlight. Try to do this in your own words rather than reading from the text
   b) Again ask the group to divide into small groups of four or five people to discuss these ideas
   c) Allow a short time for response from the groups

3. **Being Ready: This first section is divided into five chapters:**
   a) When Infatuation Passes
   b) Mourning Past Relationships
   c) Forgiveness
   d) Internet Dating
   e) Adequate Pre-Marital Counseling
   While listing all five chapters as being contained in this section, choose one chapter to highlight. After relating two or three ideas

from that chapter, again have them divide into groups and discuss what you shared.

4. **Practical Considerations; Relating to Children from the Previous Marriage; The Wedding and Support Thereafter**
Follow the same procedure used with the previous section in each of these three sections.

5. **Using *In Love Again & Making It Work* in Counseling**
   a) Choose four of the questions at the end of various chapters as examples. Read these to the group.
   b) Have the small groups discuss ways in which the book might be used with couples planning to marry again.
   c) Have each of the small groups report what they discussed.

Section-by-Section Study

In order to study the book in detail, each participant should have a copy of *In Love Again & Making It Work*. This study will be divided into five sessions.

First Session: Preface and Introduction

1. Break into small groups of four or five people. Have them share:

123

a) Name

b) One or two things about themselves

c) One question they have about remarriage

2. Choose two or three ideas from the *Preface: A Theology of Remarriage* to highlight. Try to do this in your own words rather than reading from the text.

3. Break into small groups again. Ask them to discuss what they believe about remarriage.

4. Have the small groups share together some things they talked about. What consensus can the group come to about what God thinks about divorce and remarriage

5. In the *Introduction*, Dick Dunn indicates that "most subsequent marriages fail." Share your own reaction to these words and ask the whole group to comment.

   Introduce one idea from the next session to "whet their appetites."

Second Session: Being Ready

1. This section of the book is about being ready to marry again. Since it is divided into five chapters, divide into five groups. Have each group take one of the chapters, read it over, and decide three main points to share with the other groups.

2. After deciding what the three primary ideas

of the chapter are, let the group also discuss whether or not from their own experience those are good ideas to follow. Why or why not?

3. Share the ideas from each group with the whole group.

4. In preparation for the next session, have group members choose a chapter from the next section to read before the group gets together again. Instruct each person to write down what he or she considers the main point of that chapter.

Third Session: Practical Considerations

1. Having already read a chapter from Section Two (see Second Session #4), divide the group by what chapter they read. Some groups may be larger than others. If a group is too large, divide it into two groups.

2. Since the groups have already read their chapter, let each person share what he or she thinks is the main point of that chapter. Keep a list of the various points presented.

3. Have the groups discuss what they think about the various points. Do they agree or disagree based upon their own experience?

4. Total group sharing. Let each group share the main points from their chapter and some

of their thoughts about them.

5. In preparation for the next session, assign each person a chapter to read from Section 3. You might simply have the group count off by fives.

Fourth Session: Relating to Children From the Previous Marriage

1. Since everyone was assigned a chapter to read at the last session, simply divide, joining with others who studied the same chapter.
2. This session deals with children from previous marriages. Let each person in the group share one new thing that he or she learned from reading that chapter.
3. Have each group pick one problem situation and strategize a solution.
4. Come back together as a total group. Have each sub-group share their discussion about their particular chapter.
5. Since the fifth session will be the last, ask everyone to read all five chapters before the next session.

Fifth Session: The Wedding and Support Thereafter

1. Have each person talk with his or her neighbor (in pairs) about other mistakes he or she has seen people make in terms of marrying

again. Then share those with the total group.

2. Team people up again in twos (different from the last pair). Ask them to share creative ways they have seen children involved in weddings. Share with the total group.

3. Have the total group react to the statement "People who attend a stepfamily support group can increase their chances for success from 40% to 80%." Why do they think this is so?

4. Again have people get into pairs (with different people than before). Ask them to share about how valuable they have found counseling to be. Do not ask them to share this with the total group.

5. Total group discussion: How important is a common faith or church experience in blending a family?

6. Invite closing comments concerning the study and close with prayer.